W9-CGZ-135

Dear Parents,

Welcome to the Scholastic Reader series. We have taken over 80 years of experience with teachers, parents, and children and put it into a program that is designed to match your child's interests and skills.

Level 1—Short sentences and stories made up of words kids can sound out using their phonics skills and words that are important to remember.

Level 2—Longer sentences and stories with words kids need to know and new "big" words that they will want to know.

Level 3—From sentences to paragraphs to longer stories, these books have large "chunks" of texts and are made up of a rich vocabulary.

Level 4—First chapter books with more words and fewer pictures.

It is important that children learn to read well enough to succeed in school and beyond. Here are ideas for reading this book with your child:

- Look at the book together. Encourage your child to read the title and make a prediction about the story.
- Read the book together. Encourage your child to sound out words when appropriate. When your child struggles, you can help by providing the word.
- Encourage your child to retell the story. This is a great way to check for comprehension.

Scholastic Readers are designed to support your child's efforts to learn how to read at every age and every stage. Enjoy helping your child learn to read and love to read.

—**Francie Alexander**
    Chief Education Officer
    Scholastic Education

For Ian
— F.R.

Special thanks to Paul L. Sieswerda
of The New York Aquarium
for his expertise

No part of this publication may be reproduced, or stored in a retrieval system, or transmitted in any form or by any means, electronic, mechanical, photocopying, recording, or otherwise, without written permission of the publisher. For information regarding permission, write to Scholastic Inc., Attention: Permissions Department, 557 Broadway, New York, NY 10012.

ISBN: 0-439-33015-7

Text copyright © 2003 by Fay Robinson.
Illustrations copyright © 2003 by Barbara Harmon.
All rights reserved. Published by Scholastic Inc.
SCHOLASTIC, CARTWHEEL BOOKS, and associated logos
are trademarks and/or registered trademarks of Scholastic Inc.

Library of Congress Cataloging-in-Publication Data
Robinson, Fay.
    Wacky fish! / by Fay Robinson ; illustrated by Barbara Harmon.
        p. cm. — (Scholastic reader Level 2)
    Summary: Rhyming text provides an introduction to various kinds of fish.

    ISBN 0-439-33015-7 (pbk.)
        1. Fishes—Juvenile literature. [1. Fishes.] I. Harmon, Barbara, ill.
        II. Title. III. Scholastic reader Level 2.
QL617.2 .R64 2003
597—dc21
2002006765

10 9 8 7 6 5 4 3 2 1   03 04 05 06 07
                    Printed in the U.S.A. 23 • First printing, May 2003

WACKY FISH

by **Fay Robinson**

Illustrated by **Barbara Harmon**

Scholastic Reader — Level 2

SCHOLASTIC INC. Cartwheel B·O·O·K·S ®
New York Toronto London Auckland Sydney
Mexico City New Delhi Hong Kong Buenos Aires

Gliding through our lakes and seas—

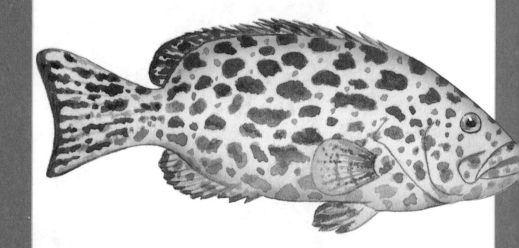

fish are awesome as can be.

You've seen lots of different fish,
but how about a fish like...

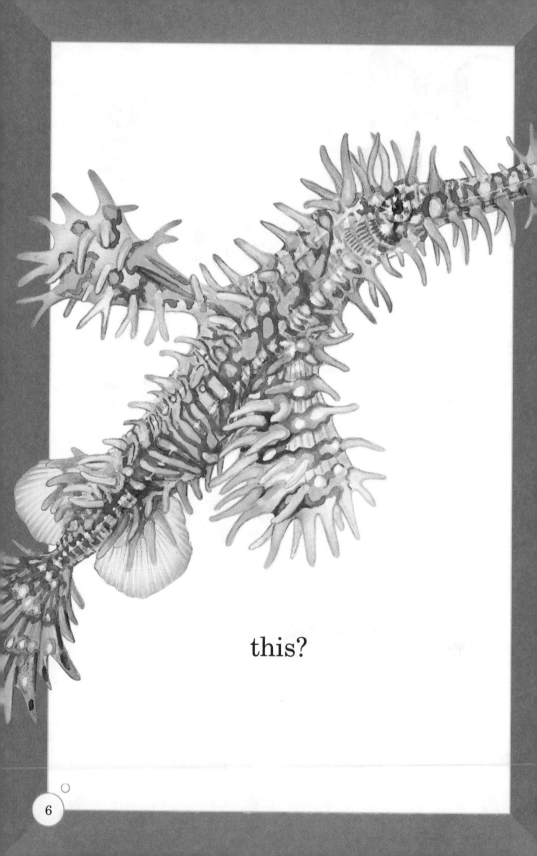

this?

Fish can look like anything—

horses,

puppets,

sticks with rings,

pancakes,

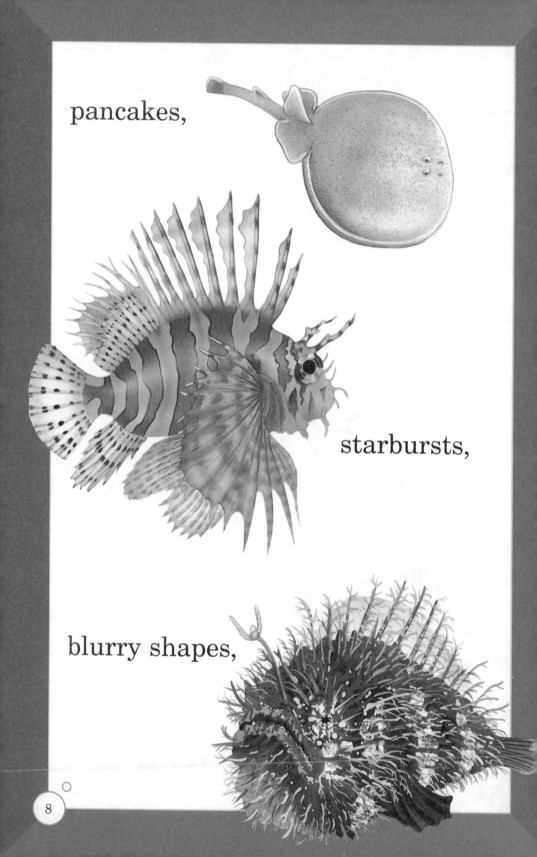

starbursts,

blurry shapes,

dragons,

serpents,

flowing capes.

Some fish look like ocean rocks.

This one's shaped just like a box.

All fish swim,
but some do more.

Many walk the ocean floor.

Some can crawl
up on the shore!

Fish with winglike fins swim by.

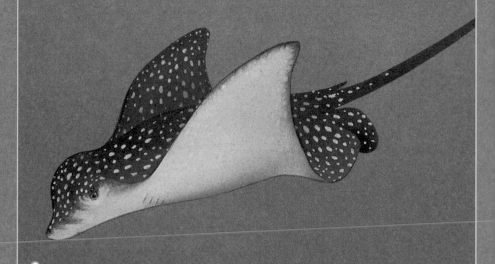

Others use their fins to fly.

Fish with humps,

fish with lumps,

fish with lots of fuzzy clumps.

Big mouths,

sad mouths,

long mouths,

mad mouths!

Danger's near!
This fish quickly...

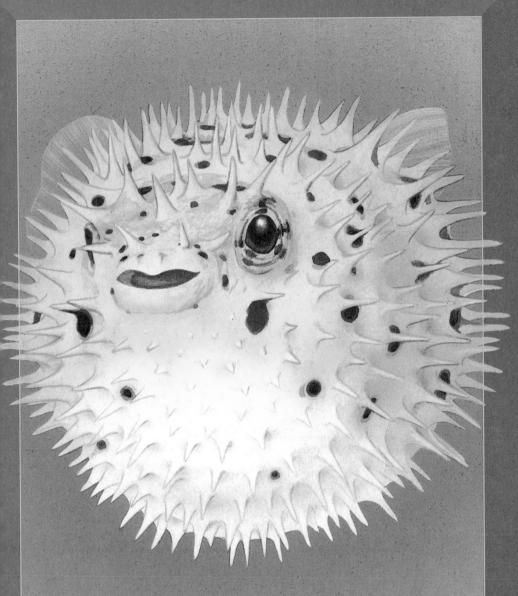

changes!
Now it's round and prickly.

Fish with spots of glowing light,

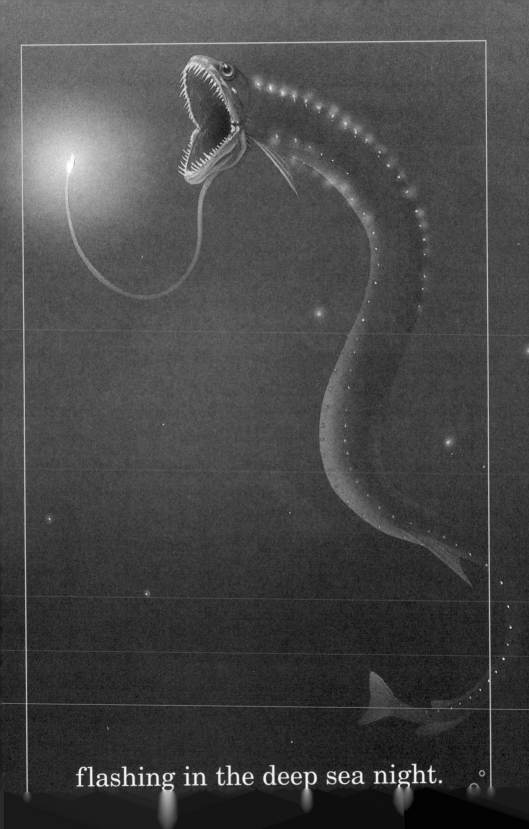

flashing in the deep sea night.

Fish have many ways to hide.
Some find holes to slide inside.

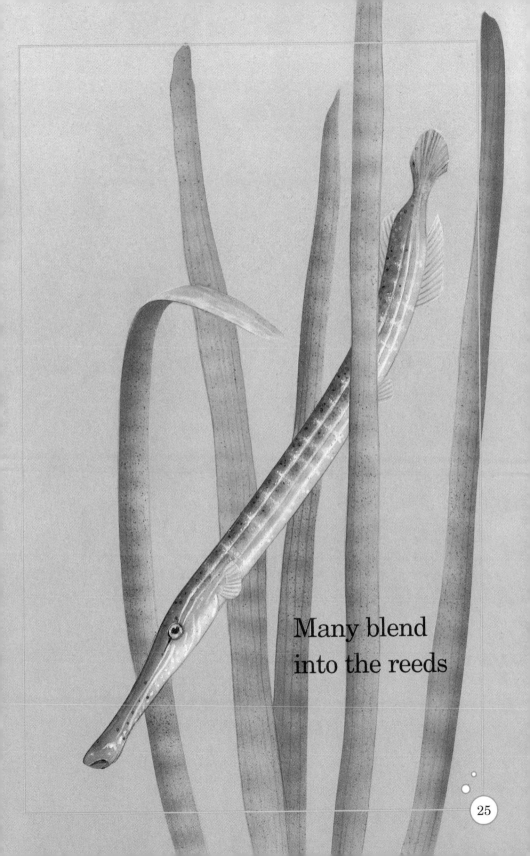

Many blend
into the reeds

or look like they are
growing weeds!

If you could dream up any fish,
would it look as strange as this?

Gliding through our lakes and seas—

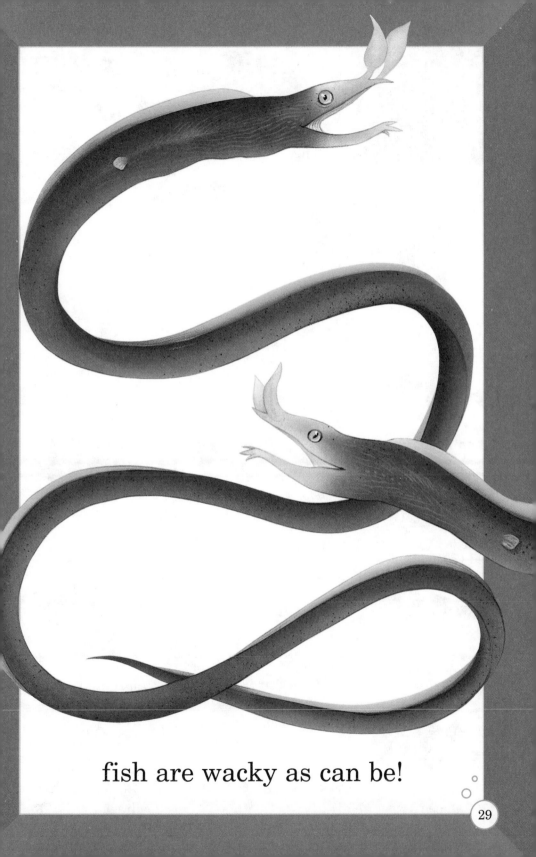

fish are wacky as can be!

Cover and page 22:
Deep Sea Anglerfish

Pages 3 and 19:
Fangtooth

Page 4:
Atlantic Mackerel

Page 4:
Red Grouper

Page 4:
Atlantic Salmon

Page 5:
Queen Triggerfish

Page 5:
Longear Sunfish

Page 5:
Central Mudminnows

Page 5:
Largemouth Bass

Page 5:
Black Bullhead

Page 6:
Ghost Pipefish

Page 7:
Sea Horse

Page 7:
Yellowmouth
Moray Eel

Page 7:
Zebra Pipefish

Page 8:
Atlantic Torpedo

Page 8:
Lionfish

Page 8:
Tassled Anglerfish

Page 9:
Weedy
Seadragon

Page 9:
Oarfish

Page 9:
Manta Ray

Page 10:
Stonefish

Page 11:
Blue Trunkfish

Page 12:
Frogfish

Page 13:
Mudskippers

Page 14:
Spotted Eagle Ray

Page 15:
Flyingfish

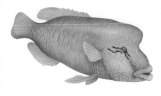

Page 16:
Humphead Wrasse

Page 16:
Lionhead Goldfish

Page 17:
Decorated Warbonnet

Page 18:
Gulper Eel

Page 18:
New Zealand
Stargazer

Page 19:
Longnose Gar

Page 20:
Porcupinefish

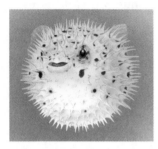

Page 21:
Porcupinefish

Page 23:
Black Seadragon

Page 24:
Blue-lined
Fangblenny

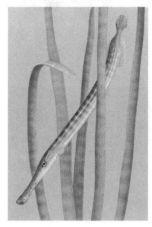

Page 25:
Trumpetfish

Page 26:
Leafy Seadragon

Page 27:
Red-lipped Batfish

Page 28:
Mola Mola
(Ocean Sunfish)

Page 29:
Ribbon Eels